A Letter

to a

Friend

A Letter

to a

Friend

The Story of Abuse in America

Patty Wain Smith

Scripture quotations are from the Revised Standard Version of The Holy Bible, copyright © 1946 and 1952 by the National Council of the Churches of Christ in the USA. Used by permission. All rights reserved.

Parts of this story have been fictionalized to protect identities and to show the common thread in their stories. It is not intended to replace consultation with a Licensed Professional Counselor, law enforcement entity, legal counsel, domestic violence assistance center or other health professional. It was written for a friend, from the author's viewpoint and life experiences, and shared to give others a better understanding of the complex dynamics in domestic violence.

New Words Publishing, 2017
ISBN-13: 978-0692825839
ISBN-10: 0692825835

Editor and designer: Nicole Smith

Dedicated to those who are made to feel powerless and defenseless.

My heartfelt thanks to the ones who've gone before me, walked beside me, or nudged me gently forward.

~

CONTENTS

INTRODUCTION
to the Letter

~

It never occurred to me she kept this kind of secret. I imagined there might have been a previous marriage, an adopted child, or a lost job buried in her past she didn't want to talk about. Everyone has baggage.

Her life seemed normal enough. She was well-kept with a nice house, cars, friends and family, including a devoted husband. Though I sensed something off the time she handed him the wrong wine glass, and he gave her an exploding glare. The fix seemed easy to me: Switch glasses. Not a big deal, I would have laughed.

I guess he didn't see it that way.

She'd become clumsy since marrying him. An odd behavior for a girl who'd played college sports and alternated between tennis and golf at the clubhouse on weekends. She wouldn't mention it unless I prodded. Only then, she'd describe bumping into a table, slipping on the stairs, or catching a tree limb in the yard. I found out after spotting bruises in unlikely places—the dressing room in an upscale boutique on a shopping trip, which happened less and less these days because he always needed her for something or another.

When he'd show up, I'd chide myself for being a selfish friend and wanting to spend time with her. I'd tell myself to give her more space. I wanted the best for her.

But when the truth came out, I wished it'd come sooner. I wished I had noticed more and given her *less* space. I wished I'd interfered long before he'd broken off our friendship and added her to the statistics.

Because in the United States, domestic violence occurs at the same rate as cesarean births and is *underreported*.[1,4] Everyone knows someone who's given birth by cesarean, but it's not easy naming victims of abuse.

Oh, they're out there.

Imagine a dinner meeting in a busy restaurant. Now count every third or fourth person and you'll get a picture of abuse happening, right here, right now, in a country we call the land of the free.

Surrounded by secrecy, the shame, embarrassment, and isolation crushes a victim's inner spirit and outer persona. The inner spirit, the abused hold onto as hard as they can. The outer persona, they hold even tighter, for they know, soon, it will be all they have. And for a woman whose husband threatens her or her children if their private family matters were ever exposed, keeping the secret is part of her survival and that of her children.

The women are different, the families are different, but the game is the same. The first one to the finish line without letting go of the secret is supposed to win.

But women playing this dangerous game, more often than not, reach the finish line way before their intended time. And sadly, many more carry their children with them until they're old enough to play the game on their own, with their own spouse and their own children, because that's what they know.

Just like now, if you're a victim, it's what you know.

The Letter

Part I

Chapter One

We Know

~

*"Be not envious of evil men, nor
desire to be with them, for their
minds devise violence, and their
lips talk of mischief."*
Proverbs 24:1-2

D ear friend,

At first the cover-up brings you guilt and shame, but after a while it takes on a life of its own like fresh paint on a canvas. You color the truth until you forget you're lying at all, and, no matter what *really* happens, you make your life appear perfect, and you fool the world or so you think.

But we know.

We know how you cry at night; we can hear your children crying too. We see the cold hatred in your husband's eyes and gaze in horror when you jump as he enters the room. We are anxious when one of your children misses school for several days after a mystery illness, in fear there was no illness, but rather marks or bruises that needed to heal lest you expose the darkness.

And we know, each time, how close you come to leaving him for your children's sake and how quickly you decide to stay, instead, "for your children's sake." And how you and your husband agree that a third party (the one you called for help) was to blame for your family's troubles.

It's in your eyes that hope is lost. It's in your voice, shaky and unsure. It's in your laugh, no longer heard, exchanged for a sound with no identity. And it's in your spirit; it has become barely recognizable.

Something that was there is gone, replaced by the shadow of who you used to be.

The Greatest of
These is Love

"But the fruit of the Spirit is love, joy, peace, patience, kindness, goodness, faithfulness, gentleness, self-control."
Galatians 5:22-23

Your children play the game with you. You are their teacher. They watch you and learn to forgive the most evil acts upon their spirits and to hold these acts in the secret chambers of their hearts, never to be opened to outsiders or to each other for that matter.

They wait and watch, nervously, with fear one hundred times your own, wondering what mood Daddy will be in when he wakes up, takes a shower or phone call, after work, during dinner, following a bad day of anything, and at every other moment in every day of their silent lives. Your children live in apprehension and fear and learn this is what love is.

You go to church as a family and sit expressionless, hearing messages of God, hope, faith, and love. You remember the words, "the greatest of these is love," but you don't know why. Your husband remembers the words, "love endures all things," and he reviews them with you and the children again and again, but you don't know why. Your youngest son asks if God really loves him. And, you don't know why.

Your husband reminds the family that, as head of the household, he must sometimes do things he doesn't want to do because he loves you so much. Your only daughter wants to know why God made love hurt so.

He tells you he's the only one who will love you after seeing, what he calls, your terrible flaws. He says your mother wants to control you, friends are jealous of your happy marriage, and everyone else has it out for him. He reminds the children you're lucky to have him, and you'd never make it without him. He tells you if you leave him there is no turning back, and he says he really means it.

He is deceiving you.

Love Rejoices
in the Right

"Love is patient and kind, love is not jealous or boastful, it does not insist on its own way, it is not irritable or resentful, it does not rejoice at wrong, but rejoices in the right."
1 Corinthians 13:4-6

These flaws he speaks of, we can't find. We see you filled with infinite gifts and possibilities, and regardless of how many times you leave us, we ask you back and truly mean it.

We are your mother, your sister, your friend, your neighbor, your children's teacher, your aunt, your grandmother (real or surrogate), and even strangers. We love you with no conditions and no demands.

We also live in fear of his explosions: the fear of losing you or your children to a physical injury he's inflicted; the fear of consequences from remedies to self-medicate so you can continue to *take it;* and the fear, that even if left physically intact, the emotional turmoil and intimidations you and your children endure might take longer than a lifetime to overcome.

We know the sound a teardrop makes as it falls from the hearts of countless angels who long to protect you. Each day, they find the way out for you, but you are too frightened to follow. Each day, they tell you of God's love for you, but you find it too good to be true. And each day, they hold you while you cry so you'll have the strength to leave, but instead, you use the strength to stay.

And God's not just sent one; he's sent so many. Some arise as strangers offering you random acts of kindness, and others, words of guidance—specific words sent by God to unsettle what you have settled for as if they know the deepest part of your being. They do.

Fear Not

"Beloved, do not believe every spirit, but test the spirits to see if they are of God."

1 John 4:1

You are in the midst of constant confusion. You, and your children, live two separate lives, and you must remember the details of each: the friends, places, phone numbers, and experiences from your life as the wife of an abuser when you choose to stay; the friends, places, phone numbers, and experiences from your life as a survivor when you choose to leave. In each case, assuring everybody it's your final decision while secretly creeping back to the other side to see if maybe you should turn around after all.

On top of this fence you walk, balancing carefully so you don't have to commit to either side. On one side, you are the devoted wife of a batterer: fearful, desperate, but belonging to something you believe to be greater than yourself, something you are familiar with. On the other side, you still see enough of your goodness to want to salvage what he's failed to destroy and failed to silence. What remains within you is due to something greater than yourself, but it is not he.

He is not all-powerful. He is not all knowing. He is not God. He is simply a human being with a powerful problem that's not within your control to change. Only he can do this, and he hasn't.

With each word, with each look, with each action and reaction, he makes a choice to behave abusively. He could tell you he needs to take a walk around the block, and do it, or ask to be left alone until he's rational and calm, but he does not.

Any attempts by him to change have been grand gestures that are short-lived. He's been to counseling with you (and the children) a half dozen times or more, each lasting only several months because he says he's changed. He says he's read every book you've bought, borrowed, and checked out for him, and he really gets it.

He sounds convincing when he explains to those close to you why it's not his fault and how things are better now. He speaks in a kind voice you don't recognize that puts a cold shiver in your heart.

He is a stranger.

Chapter Two
Trapped

~

"A new heart I will give you, and a new spirit I will put within you."
Ezekiel 36:26

He is a stranger to your mind. You remember the kindness he showed you once, when you first dated, but you can't hold the memory longer than an instant. It becomes like a favorite forgotten song, a jeweled shell tossed about in a wave, you cannot hold onto. And although brief and distant, you long for those moments. They become just enough to sustain you. They are your *drug-of-choice.*

So you remain on this path, and as you sit, he races toward you, his headlights beaming brighter and brighter soon to topple you. Surely you must see him coming. You do not, your eyes are shut.

Someone shouts, "Get up, get up!"

But it's too late. It is over. An unnatural silence hangs in the air. Emergency crews arrive at the scene, but there's nothing they can do. They cover your face with a simple white sheet: If only you had opened your eyes.

Pulling your arm, your little girl wakes you to silence the screams. It's just another dream—this time.

He is a stranger to your body. So mindful is he of his own needs and desires, and his own inadequacies, that he cannot see past them to give love for love's sake. The gentle touch, the caring glance, the genuine exchange of warm human emotion, he does not know.

He can't comprehend giving without a reason, without a return or manipulation imposed. He knows love only as a feeling or lack of, needing to be filled, needing to be had, and needing to be possessed. Without it, he believes he is powerless, and to him that is less than nothing.

He is a stranger to your heart. His burden has you so broken, so worn, so troubled. You search his love for some semblance of affection or admiration, nothing complicated or complex, just true. You look for this proof in every word, every sound and every image, real or imagined.

It's as if you're married to two men now. One man, kind and gentle, arrives for short periods when least expected and just in time to convince you to stay. But the other man is the one most present now, and he brings a myriad of formidable encounters you try to avoid with unmistakable effort and concentration, a skill in which you have become well practiced.

Your sacrifices, your martyrdom, he cannot begin to appreciate. How could he?

He has no real sense of the anguish he inflicts upon your spirit, but that does not make it alright—only unfixable.

From Where He Sits

"By wisdom a house is built, and by understanding it is established; by knowledge the rooms are filled with all the precious and pleasant riches. A wise man is mightier than a strong man, and a man of knowledge than he who has strength."
Proverbs 24:3-5

You are the keeper of his kingdom and the peacemaker of his soul. He requires no less than continuous, unconditional reassurances of your loyalty at all times and in all places. He watches your every breath, your every move. He has to. His continued existence increasingly befalls your shoulders.

He must be certain of his emotional safety, and he holds you accountable—accountable for

HIS past, accountable for HIS present, and accountable for HIS future—yet he allows you limited participation. All this he does for the feeling that he is *something.* He must remain in control, not of himself, of others and most specifically, of you.

He knows of your kindness, your gentleness, your understanding and most notably, your forgiveness: He counts on it, and he wouldn't want it any other way, for it wouldn't work any other way.

"It must be!" is his mantra.

He takes what he needs as he needs it. He deserves these things, he believes, without explanation or sacrifice nor sweat or toil. It is his entitlement.

He recalls to you his father laying down the law and reminding Mom who's boss. "That's the way it's always been," he claims. He and his siblings were respectful of their father's authority, his vengeance. They made themselves scarce whenever he was home from work at night or on the weekend, and after work, his father went on regular outings with *the boys.* They were relieved they didn't see him much, thankful really.

He remembers his mother disagreeing with his father, at times, followed by her absence for several days and a visit to a friend's house or the hospital. "My poor father," he explains, "Mom was sick a lot and too emotional. He says he only stayed with her because he's a great guy and someone had to take care of her."

He doesn't know what he comes from or its influence, and he doesn't want to know. He won't acknowledge the grief and pain that trespassed against him because he can't bear it. So like you now, he created a new story, a new memory.

But you are not the same, you are not even close, you are not the abuser.

This is *his* battle. This is the demon he fights—the daily abominations of his heart and mind. He lives in chaos difficult to define and believes he can never be delivered. He feels no self-responsibility, and so he makes the best of it.

And he thinks you, like he, deserve your lot; it's nothing personal. From where he sits, it's just the way things are like a shuffling of cards, a playing of hands, or a dealing of fates.

And yet, he finds no rest.

The Plan

"For I know the plans I have for you, says the Lord, plans for welfare and not for evil, to give you a future and a hope."

Jeremiah 29:11

Where he goes, you cannot follow, for it is a place in the depths of darkness, barely illuminated by the Spirit. Someone once told you of this dark, barren wasteland, but you were not sure it really existed. A black hole, a soundless century-long existence few ever return from, few can ever bear.

You cry for him, his circumstance; you suffer and anguish over his decided present and future, but you cannot change it, and you must go on.

He would want that for you, a victory in some sense, and he would want that for his children because deep inside his soul a hint of compassion remains. Hard to find, it is there nevertheless, buried beneath years of neglect and desperation.

He will deny it, he fears it—to him it is a weakness, his Achilles heel—because he knows that minute bit of humanity, that sliver of light, could be his downfall and bring your escape.

You must take it.

Your energies and reflections have been focused on him. Even in sleep, you're reminded of your daily encounters. Exhausted, your resources strained, you are repeatedly ill with viruses, headaches and other maladies, many which can't be named (but exist nonetheless).

Your body reminds you of the costly toll it pays to defend itself, to prepare for the worst, to live with the enemy. And now, your tolerance weakened, your immunity impaired, he is at his worst, and you must fight to survive, to escape.

The role he assigned you, you once accepted graciously. But now you must reassess your assignment and uncover your real responsibility.

This is your purpose. This is your stronghold.

Father!

"I sought the Lord, and he answered me, and delivered me from all my fears."

Psalms 34:4

You question your circumstances like a lost child on the first day of school and stare at the gift God left when your husband first became two people. Sitting by the bedside table close to your Bible, the brilliantly wrapped box addressed to you with love arrived soon after you prayed for his healing.

You imagine what's inside and want to open it, but you are afraid. You're frightened of the answer it may reveal, frightened of the truth it may disclose, and frightened of the sacrifice it may require. It's been waiting a long time for your attention, yet you've put it off for another day, another time, another...

It can wait no longer. The time is now, your escape is now. You must raise your children far from this turmoil, far from this taker of light, this hardener of hearts, so they can experience the warmth of the sun's rays upon their hearts, minds, and bodies. This is why they were created, to give and receive the highest love, the greatest compassion, the most wonderful dreams. Move them to higher ground, quickly, without hesitation or looking back.

Open the gift.
It is for you.

You think about the gifts your husband's given you: the flowers after he accused you, belittled you, broke your heart; the dinner and wine after he broke the door or the wall; the jewelry and thoughtful cards after he pushed you or pulled you or hurt you in a number of other unmentionable ways.

Afterward the payoff is wonderful, magical even: candlelight, kisses, caresses like a princess in a fairy tale. He retreats like a small boy who accidentally broke his mother's favorite vase, always sorry. But then it is gone, and his sweetness, his sympathy, his compassion disappears into the darkness and into hiding.

The escalation, the buildup, begins again for the next time and the next. *Each time's* worse than the last—and you are tired.

You pick up the gift.

And as you hold it, you hear your husband's steely voice, in an echo, warning you about gifts from strangers. God's not a stranger, is he?

You try to recall when you last talked to God, confided in him, trusted him. You wonder when you turned away, believing you did not deserve his promises and putting your husband, instead, in God's place.

Breaking down, you fall to your knees, and the unopened gift tumbles from your hands.

You cry out, "Father!"

You reach your arms toward the sky like a toddler wanting to be carried, wanting to be held, and later, lovingly placed down in the right direction. You see, clearly, God had never left your side, but it was you who wouldn't look at him, ashamed of what you'd become.

You cry for what seems like eternity with tears from a well deepened by grief. You cry not only for yourself, you cry for women everywhere, past, present, and future. These are the tears that will cleanse your soul; these are the tears that will elevate your spirit; and these are the cries heard, even unto the heavens, unto your Father.

God has heard your cries. And he has answered them.

Chapter Three
The Gift

~

"But they who wait for the Lord shall renew their strength, they shall mount up with wings like eagles, they shall run and not be weary, they shall walk and not faint."

Isaiah 40:31

After the last tear fell, there was a calm, a stillness that left peace in your heart, a place where misery and despair had resided. It's nothing less than miraculous, this transformation, and like the turning of a page, the suffering is over, the weight lifted.

You feel weak, shaken, bruised by a past not so far behind you, but you feel anticipation for the future and hope. *Hope.* Thinking softly about it, your smile grows; there's a promise within it for you and your children.

And so, knowing it's time to open the gift God left by the bedside table, the one brilliantly wrapped and addressed to you with love, you reach for it without hesitation, encouraged it's what you need.

You open the gift.
It is what you need.

God-given, pure, and free, the powerful gift celebrates your humanness, keeps you safe, and changes darkness into light; and it's yours, dear friend. Inside the box is a scroll, and the inscription reads:

C-H-O-I-C-E

Take your power. Take your freedom and God's gift for you. It can change your reality and fill your dreams because each step is your choice, each day is your journey, and each success is your victory. You can choose your circumstances; that's the gift.

And it is your responsibility to choose wisely just as it's your responsibility to choose again when you don't, and that time will come, for no one is perfect. Don't be afraid to admit your mistakes, understand it's alright to be wrong, and move forward.

The cycle of abuse is in your hands to continue or not. You have the power to free generations of children and adults, and yourself. No one will assume your responsibility because no one can.

Like a field of baseball players, there's only one at bat: IT IS YOU. The cycle's calling you—every hour and every minute—pleading, "Your turn. Your move. Your decision."

What will you do?

Part II

Chapter Four
No More!

~

"I can do all things in him who strengthens me."
Philippians 4:13

You awaken early one morning. The sun flickers through your curtains like a cache of butterflies out on a morning flight. You'd said your goodbye, he's not there. And for the first time in years, you feel rested, content, self-assured, and just plain good.

A metamorphosis has taken place, a restoration—you know that, there's no doubt—and you are happy to be on the other side, grateful to have survived.

You made your decision, you gave your answer, you presented your choice. But it's not over, he's stopping by to talk. You don't want to talk, you have nothing more to say, and you feel good today.

When he called, he made you promise. "You owe me that much," he'd said. After the call, you vowed to not let it spoil this great day, and besides, you already told him you were through. You figured you'd have a quick talk and things would be over with, settled, and then you could get on with your life.

But you know it's never that simple with him, never that easy. He can't just let go, not without a fight, not without being the winner.

You wonder, "Where is he staying? What is he doing? Does he want to see the children or just me?" Your chest tightens, you feel dizzy. Breathing in and out, it passes.

Your daughter runs into the room. "When is Daddy coming?" Laughing, she bounces on the bed.

You show her the time on the clock and help her get ready, putting her in a little girl's dress (the one his mother gave her) and combing her hair.

You look for the bow that matches, and when you can't find it, you panic. "Where is it?" Searching the drawer, behind the dresser, in the closet, you cry.

"Mommy," your daughter tugs on you. "Bows are for babies. I'm a big girl."

With dripping tears, you give her a warm squeeze. "You are a big girl."

After wiping your face, you shake your head, and sigh. You can't believe the power you give him, and promise, "No more!"

You take your daughter back to her room, hang up the dress, and dig out other possibilities. You smile. "What would you like to wear?"

Her young eyes widen; she can't remember picking before. She heads for the neon blue shirt with the matching belt and bell-bottomed blue jeans.

"My sister's," you whisper.

Holding them in front of her, she dances across the room. She twirls around like a new bird on its first flight, and says, "I can be a model."

You tell her, "You can be anything."

Revelation

"Now the Lord is the Spirit, and where the Spirit of the Lord is, there is freedom."

2 Corinthians 3:17

The doorbell rings, and when you peek out the window, you see him standing there groomed and shined. He arrives early, intentionally, to catch you off-guard, and appears in a pressed shirt with polished shoes, a new haircut, and a clean-shaven face.

You call to the backyard, "Boys, your dad's here," and the doorbell rings again as the boys hurry in.

At the front door, you twist clumsily at the knob before it opens to the man on the stoop. He's got your favorite flowers tight within his grasp, and you smell the aftershave he saves for special occasions on his face.

Looking at you tenderly, he says, "Can I come in?" as he steps inside.

The scene he purposely set (and you once longed for) doesn't work anymore. Sadly, you see him as a lost soul, a remorseless being. You still fear him: That will never change. But you won't act out of fear of him. You won't go back to that nightmare, and you won't take your children there. You no longer admire him, look up to him, or think he is greater than another, and you will never trust him again, ever.

He clears his throat, sensing he does not have your full attention, and tells you how sorry he is for *everything*.

You watch him like an audience watches a performer, studying his motions, his eyes, and his face, but you say nothing. You are outside of it now. Even as he tries to bring you back into the game, you refuse to participate, and without you, it cannot continue.

What a revelation!

Your daughter slips into the room, and he falls silent. With a running jump, she lands in his arms, and asks, "Do you like my outfit, Daddy?"

Recognizing it, he inhales deep, surprised to see her dressed in what he swore she'd never wear.

She asks again, "Do you, Daddy? Do you?"

"Sure," he says, and quietly berates himself for not getting there sooner.

Flying by the entryway, the boys freeze when they spot their dad, and noting it, he rubs his chin and smiles. When he gets to them, he makes a mess of their hair, and he reassures himself that he's still in command.

But he is sorely mistaken.

The Storm

"Then they cried to the Lord in their trouble, and he delivered them from their distress; he made the storm be still, and the waves of the sea were hushed."

Psalms 107:28-29

Beware. This he can't handle, that someone other than he would stop the game that validates his existence. He is the umpire, the scorekeeper, and the rule-maker, he believes; and he decides when the game begins and when, if ever, it ends. Like a bully on a playground, he believes it's his place to rule whomever he perceives is weaker, and he thinks it's your place to remember.

The war is on, and he will not share the rules of engagement. He couldn't, even if he wanted to, because he constantly changes them to suit his needs and requirements as he sees fit, as he feels is necessary to win, always.

But he has, this time, underestimated your resolve, your fortitude, and your courage. He has underestimated the determination of your spirit to live as it was intended, in freedom. And he has underestimated your love for your children—this mountain you *will* move for them, even as he tests you and stretches you to your limits and threatens to harm you.

You must understand, by now, that your continued interactions with him leave you in serious danger, not only from spiritual assaults, but also from physical harm to your body. You must understand that in this time of separation from him, you're at your greatest risk, in your greatest peril, as he is in his deepest distress.

Be on your most reverent guard, and do not underestimate his desperation. Take the precautions and warnings from those who've traveled the road, for they've seen the enemy and know him by name.

Listen to their account of the survivors, and believe it when they say the only thing more dangerous than leaving today is leaving tomorrow because each day brings an added and greater risk to you and your children. And know, not leaving is the most dangerous choice of all.

If you turn back, he'll steal your hope without warning or thought. He'll batter your heart like a storm set on destroying the very rocks that sustain its waters. And he'll alter your spirit into the likeness of the deep where only the slightest sound is heard, the faintest light is seen.

And your children will follow.

There is real danger and one way out: the safest path. Your house is crumbling before you, it is falling to the ground, and though you may be injured on the way out, you will surely perish if you stay, and it is your duty to try.

It is your responsibility to survive.

Chapter Five
The Seven Sorrows

~

*"Trust in the Lord, with all your heart,
and do not rely on your own insight.
In all your ways acknowledge him,
and he will make straight your paths."*
Proverbs 3:5-6

Nobody can predict when he'll tire of the games he brings before you. Therefore, you must prepare for his bribes and illusions, and remember they're merely deceits from a clever imposter. Prepare for more threats and intimidations because they too will come.

Your armor must be strong, your resistance sound, your feet firmly planted—and you must maintain it. Still, you are free, your children are free, and it is well worth the preparations.

If you're ever tempted to go back to him, think about The Seven Sorrows. Learn it, memorize it—use it as a shield, and truth as a sword, and don't be overcome.

The Seven Sorrows

1. Your children have no mother.
   Their father killed her.

2. Your children can't see their father.
   He is now in jail.

3. Your children have no father.
   Their mother killed him in self-defense.

4. Your children can't see their mother.
   She is now in jail.

5. Your children have a mother.
   They never know her beauty.

6. Your son has a wife.
   She says he abuses her.

7. Your daughter has a husband.
   She says she fell.

Chapter Six
The Way Home

~

"And you will know the truth, and the truth will make you free."
John 8:32

It's a long way home, but God makes good shoes. You're not sure where you heard that, but you hold it like a lifeline passed to you just before your descent. You know where to place your trust now, you know where to put your faith—a lesson learned the hard way that's learned just the same.

And you are the greater for it somehow; your humility and compassion are even more enhanced.

You embrace it as evidence of your humanness, but you do not expend it on the abuser. Your cause has become new.

It is for you. It is for your children. It is for thousands, the group you once denied belonging to: those who are made to feel powerless and defenseless, those whose freedoms have been extorted. This is where your sympathy lies. This is where your devotion sets. This is where your motivation carries. And this is where you'll be given your surety of freedom.

In serving this group, you'll receive daily reminders of the plight, the degradation, and the enslavement of the human spirit—and you'll be sure not to go there again. You'll learn to recognize it, and if it calls your name, you'll hear danger, and if it sends you falsehoods, you'll see lies.

Stay on this path, focus on the smallest of miracles and know you are free. There is truly no greater miracle than freedom, no greater possession, and no higher desire. It's from freedom that we're born, and it's into freedom that we'll die.

It is our natural state and our desired berth:

How then, can one presume to deny or take from another the most basic human right?

And though we live in a free society, some are bound anyway, and we cannot afford to take freedom for granted, for its value is too high, and its loss is too great. And because without it, happiness will not grow, wellness will not propagate, and promise will not supply.

At times, we must make a claim and safeguard its survival for ourselves. Other times, we must fight the demons that conspire to entrap others, and make a claim too.

Guard it closely.

Words For Living

*"Oh that you would bless me indeed,
and enlarge my territory, that your
hand would be with me, and that you
would keep me from evil, that
I may not cause pain!"*
1 Chronicles 4:10

Healing takes time, but that doesn't mean you have to stay in a critically wounded place. Many would consider you lucky to survive, but I call you blessed, protected, and loved beyond the edge of the universe where God lives. And so, I pray your lessons are swift, your healing is complete, and your home is built with genuine love.

For although we stumble, we can rebound

and recover because that's how we are made. We have self-healing properties, and since we can learn from our mistakes, it helps to understand their causes.

Remember, there's considerable power in words, and strength to indignation. Take care each day, consider these affirmations, and start your own.

Affirmations

1. **Acknowledge the problem.**
   Admit to emotional or physical danger.

2. **Ask for help.**
   We all need it sooner or later.

3. **Trust your instincts.**
   Fear is a survival instinct.

4. **Listen to what's revealed.**
   Pay very close attention.

5. **Past behavior predicts future behavior.**
   Insurance companies rely on it.

6. **Don't marry potential.**
   People are patterns of behavior.

7. **What you focus on, you create.**
   Start with the smallest of miracles.

8. **It's okay to be wrong.**
   Choose again.

9. **Love isn't just a feeling.**
   It's how you treat someone.

Chapter Seven
Permission to Love

~

"And if I have prophetic powers, and understand all mysteries and all knowledge, and if I have all faith, so as to remove mountains, but have not love, I am nothing."

1 Corinthians 13:2

You have been through a great storm, an unspeakable journey, and you have survived. That should give you some idea of what God made you to be and of who you are. You are a survivor and the heroine of your children's present and future. Not only have you demonstrated your great courage and love for them, but you've also taught them how to make difficult choices, showing them where to draw the line on how they will be treated.

Now, as before, you teach them about life and the world around them, but this time you teach them to love themselves and to value themselves. And most importantly, you give them permission to give and receive love, and expect it—as it should be.

Years may pass before the scars inside heal, and some may never heal, but you will love each other right through it. Already you feel the light increasing in your hearts with warmth you had nearly forgotten: the simple feeling of peace, a quiet stillness that requires no material possessions or sounds to illustrate, and above all, love.

Your children debut smiles new to you with optimism and grace. They laugh and dance like fairies, and with their magic wands, they command, "Anything is possible, anything!"

Giggling, they run to the edge of the room with different dress-up clothes each time, and when their faces light up, true happiness splashes from their eyes. With anticipation, your own face beams when they invite you into their make-believe land.

You go willingly, appreciative of the time and the opportunity. Falling on the floor, laughing, from something they've said, they pile on top, tickling you. As you hug and kiss them (and they you), it's hard to believe you lived any other way.

And yes, being away from their daddy, they'll be sad at times; it's only natural. But they're thankful for this miracle, their new freedom, permission to love themselves and each other, and peacefulness.

Their worries are now of child-like proportion: What should I wear to school? How much homework do I have? What are we having for dinner? When can we leave for the birthday party? Will they have ice cream?

These are the worries of childhood as they should be. And they are enough.

Teach Your Children

"Let the children come to me, do not hinder them, for to such belongs the kingdom of God."

Mark 10:14

Teach your children well, for God loves them as he loves you. You can't keep them from every ill of the world since that would mean perfection, and it cannot be achieved in the world as we know it now. But carry their spirits diligently, carefully, and lovingly because one day they'll become guardians of this world, and the people in it, and they'll use our teachings to shape the future of all humanity.

Love them dearly and gently, teach them consistently but tenderly, and keep them in the light of God's love, now and always. That will be your greatest gift to them.

Teach them to love and be loved. Teach them that although it's better to give, it's also important to receive; show them they have value and worth that could never be replaced or forgotten; remind them they're unique human beings who've been purposefully made; and tell them just how lucky you feel to have them.

Remember to love yourself as God loves you, and, at every step and at every age, there's a purpose for your life. Understand his ways are of a higher dimension than ours, and you may never know the details or the reasons.

And trust him. Like a child being warned of a hot stove, you must trust your Father, for he sees where you cannot, and he always has a plan for you. Talk with him, confide in him, and ask him for direction, and when you're ready, pray he'll open your heart to love again.

Then, in the twilight of your human experience, remember the lessons of love and courage; remember your angels. Above all, remember the gift God gave you when you were broken and afraid, the one brilliantly wrapped and addressed to you with love, left by the bedside table to use throughout your life.

Use it well, dear friend.

Today is a new day, and it will be more glorious than ever before in a way you have never known. Thank God for this day, bask in its glory, dance with the fairies, and dream—because all fairies know, "Anything is possible, anything!"

POSTSCRIPT
to the Letter

~

"Peace I leave with you, my peace I give to you, not as the world gives do I give to you. Let not your hearts be troubled, neither let them be afraid."
John 14:27

The next time you imagine a dinner meeting in a busy restaurant, look around, notice the faces, feel the dreams. No, don't forget the statistics; be present for someone in need. But realize there's a miracle in all of us: every living, breathing, and heart-beating soul. It doesn't matter who you are—we are the same. Hope is placed where we need it, and it will find you.

Live in peace, my friend.

STATISTICS

Over the last 20 years, The Hotline and loveisrespect have answered more than 4 million calls, chats and texts from people seeking help around issues of domestic violence and dating abuse. [7]

More than 1 in 3 women (35.6%) and more than 1 in 4 men (28.5%) in the United States have experienced rape, physical violence and/or stalking by an intimate partner in their lifetime. [1]

Centers for Disease Control and Prevention reports the Cesarean Delivery Rate for the year 2013 at 32.7%. [4]

Nearly half of all women and men in the United States have experienced psychological aggression by an intimate partner in their lifetime (48.4% and 48.8%, respectively). [1]

Intimate partner violence alone affects more than 12 million people each year. [1]

From 1994 to 2010, about 4 in 5 victims of intimate partner violence were female. [5]

Nearly half (43%) of dating college women report experiencing violent and abusive dating behaviors. [2]

1.5 million high school students nationwide experience physical abuse from a dating partner in a single year. [6]

Domestic violence is prevalent in every community and affects all people regardless of age, socioeconomic status, sexual orientation, gender, race, religion, or nationality. [3]

According to the Report of the American Psychological Association Presidential Task Force on Violence and the Family:

"A child's exposure to the father abusing the mother is the strongest risk factor for transmitting violent behavior from one generation to the next." [8]

BIBLIOGRAPHY

[1] Black, M. C., Basile, K. C., Breiding, M. J., Smith, S. G., Walters, M. L., Merrick, M. T., ... Stevens, M. R. (2011). *The National Intimate Partner and Sexual Violence Survey (NISVS): 2010 Summary Report* (Rep.). Atlanta, GA: National Center for Injury Prevention and Control, Centers for Disease Control and Prevention.

[2] *College Dating Violence and Abuse Poll* (Rep.). (2011, June). Retrieved Spring, 2017, from Fifth & Pacific Companies, Inc. (Formerly Liz Claiborne, Inc.), Conducted by Knowledge Networks website: www.breakthecycle.org/surveys

[3] *Domestic Violence National Statistics* (Rep.). (2015). Retrieved Spring, 2017, from National Coalition Against Domestic Violence website: www.ncadv.org

[4] Martin, J. A., Hamilton, B. E., Osterman, M. K., & E. (2015). *Births: Final Data for 2013. National vital statistics reports* (Vol. 64, Rep. No. 1). Hyattsville, MD: National Center for Health Statistics.

[5] *November 2012 Special Report* (Rep.). (n.d.). Retrieved Spring, 2017, from Bureau of Justice Statistics website: www.bjs.gov/index.cfm?ty=pbdetail&iid=4536

[6] *Physical Dating Violence Among High School Students - United States, 2003, Morbidity and Mortality Weekly Report* (Vol. 55, Rep. No. 19). (2006). Atlanta, GA: Centers for Disease Control and Prevention.

[7] *The National Domestic Violence Hotline* (Rep.). (2016). Retrieved Spring, 2017, from www.thehotline.org/wp-content/uploads/2017/03/2016-Impact-Report.pdf

[8] *Violence and the family: Report of the American Psychological Association Presidential Task Force on Violence and the Family* (Rep.). (1996). Washington, DC: American Psychological Association.

REVIEWS

"Excellent! A dark story told with deep insight. Gripping. Beautifully written. Told like it is. First rate work!"

David Zinman
Author (The Day Huey Long Was Shot)
Prize-winning AP Journalist/Newsday Reporter

"Standing ovation. Simply amazing!"

"*A Letter to a Friend* is an extremely emotional and gripping read! Domestic violence is not only about horrific acts that leave bumps, bruises, scars, broken bones...and occasionally even death. Patty Wain Smith does an incredible job depicting how abuse takes more than a physical toll on victims, but strong emotional and psychological tolls, as well! This book gives the reader a clear and deep understanding of what abuse truly looks like. It is given a face, and the reader is part of the story.

As a therapist, I have worked with hundreds of people impacted by abuse. *A Letter to a Friend* gives the reader a true look inside the minds of so many. The feelings of isolation and fear are immobilizing for many victims. I feel very strongly this book can aid and empower victims, ultimately helping them to transition from victims to survivors."

Leah M. Leuthauser, MA, LPC

"As a professional counselor and educator for over thirty years, directing a mental health center and teaching on a graduate and undergraduate level, I have had the opportunity to witness first-hand some of the terrible consequences of domestic abuse. Domestic abuse is a problem that crosses all social and cultural lines and impacts on everyone, not only the victim of abuse, but children who themselves may get caught up in this terrible cycle of abuse.

Many years ago, I was fortunate to have Patty Smith as one of my students and I had foreseen her potential to be an excellent teacher or counselor who could make a very strong impact on the lives of others. As I read *A Letter to a Friend*, I feel she has more than exceeded my expectations.

As I perused each passage of *A Letter to a Friend*, I found it to be moving and insightful with a powerful message not only for the victim of abuse—but a message that transcends to anyone who cares about the circumstances of those who are caught up in this terrible web of abuse.

I strongly recommend *A Letter to a Friend* to everyone; and especially to those who need to read its message and comprehend their need to empower themselves to take the steps necessary to break the cycle."

Dr. James W. Pearson, ACSW, LPC

The National Domestic
Violence Hotline

1-800-799-SAFE (7233)
1-800-787-3224 (TTY)

Listen to the song Each Time by Patty Wain Smith at:
www.youtube.com/watch?v=sIXnlfGz_o4

If you found **A Letter to a Friend** helpful, please help others find it by leaving a review.

1. Visit: www.amazon.com/author/pattywainsmith

2. Click on **A Letter to a Friend: The Story of Abuse in America—Print Edition.**

3. Scroll down to **Customer Reviews** and click **Write a Customer Review.**

Thank you for reading A Letter to a Friend: The Story of Abuse in America.

Made in the USA
Monee, IL
18 August 2020